POLICE FORCE CAREERS

HEATHER C. HUDAK

CRABTREE
PUBLISHING COMPANY
WWW.CRABTREEBOOKS.COM

CRABTREE
PUBLISHING COMPANY
WWW.CRABTREEBOOKS.COM

Author: Heather C. Hudak
Editors: Sarah Eason
Jennifer Sanderson
Ellen Rodger
Proofreader: Tracey Kelly
Indexer: Tracey Kelly
Editorial director:
Kathy Middleton
Interior design: Emma DeBanks
Cover and logo design:
Katherine Berti
Photo research: Rachel Blount
Print coordinator:
Katherine Berti
Consultant: David Hawksett

Written, developed, and produced for Crabtree Publishing by Calcium Creative Ltd.

Photo Credits:
t=Top, tr=Top Right, tl=Top Left
Inside: Dreamstime.com: Angela Ostafichuk: p. 15; Shutterstock: ACHPF: pp. 1, 9; Bibiphoto: p. 21; Edi Chen: p. 11; Couperfield: pp. 17, 19; Gorodenkoff: p. 24; Dan Holm: p. 8; A. Katz: p. 5; KellyNelson: p. 20; LightField Studios: p. 25; Monkey Business Images: p. 27; Nic Neufeld: p. 12; Silent O: pp. 3, 28b; Alexander Oganezov: p. 13; Pho.stories: p. 4; John Roman Images: p. 28t; J. Robert Williams: p. 6; Leonard Zhukovsky: p. 29; Zoka74: p. 16; Wikimedia Commons: Marc Cooper: pp. 7, 23. Front cover: Shutterstock

---

Library and Archives Canada Cataloguing in Publication

Title: Police force careers / Heather C. Hudak.
Names: Hudak, Heather C., 1975- author.
Description: Series statement: Careers on the front line | Includes bibliographical references and index.
Identifiers: Canadiana (print) 2020028391X | Canadiana (ebook) 20200283928 | ISBN 9780778781417 (hardcover) | ISBN 9780778781479 (softcover) | ISBN 9781427125811 (HTML)
Subjects: LCSH: Police—Vocational guidance—United States—Juvenile literature. | LCSH: Police—Vocational guidance—Canada—Juvenile literature.
Classification: LCC HV7922 .H83 2020 | DDC j363.2/2—dc23

Library of Congress Cataloging-in-Publication Data

Names: Hudak, Heather C., 1975- author.
Title: Police force careers / Heather C. Hudak.
Description: New York : Crabtree Publishing Company, [2021] | Series: Careers on the front line | Includes index.
Identifiers: LCCN 2020029711 (print) | LCCN 2020029712 (ebook) | ISBN 9780778781417 (hardcover) | ISBN 9780778781479 (paperback) | ISBN 9781427125811 (ebook)
Subjects: LCSH: Police--Vocational guidance--Juvenile literature. | Police--Juvenile literature. | Law enforcement--Vocational guidance--Juvenile literature.
Classification: LCC HV7922 .H83 2021 (print) | LCC HV7922 (ebook) | DDC 363.2092/273--dc23
LC record available at https://lccn.loc.gov/2020029711
LC ebook record available at https://lccn.loc.gov/2020029712

Crabtree Publishing Company
www.crabtreebooks.com   1-800-387-7650

Printed in the U.S.A./082020/CG20200710

Copyright © **2021 CRABTREE PUBLISHING COMPANY.** All rights reserved. No part of this publication may be reproduced, stored in a retrieval system, or be transmitted in any form or by any means, electronic, mechanical, photocopying, recording, or otherwise, without the prior written permission of Crabtree Publishing Company. In Canada: We acknowledge the financial support of the Government of Canada through the Canada Book Fund for our publishing activities.

Published in Canada
Crabtree Publishing
616 Welland Ave.
St. Catharines, Ontario
L2M 5V6

Published in the United States
Crabtree Publishing
347 Fifth Ave
Suite 1402-145
New York, NY 10016

Published in the United Kingdom
Crabtree Publishing
Maritime House
Basin Road North, Hove
BN41 1WR

Published in Australia
Crabtree Publishing
3 Charles Street
Coburg North
VIC, 3058

CONTENTS

Protecting People 4
A Frontline Career 6
Frontline Patrolling 8
Patrol Stories Andrew Youssef: Horseback-Riding Hero 10
In the Community 12
Community Stories Sergeant Chris Laush: Breaking Cultural Barriers ... 14
Investigating Crime 16
Investigator Stories Detective Joe Kenda: Homicide Hunter 18
Special Operations 20
Special Op Stories Jennifer Grasso: SWAT Superstar 22
Behind the Front Line 24
Support Stories Anastacia Byrne: Saving Lives with Words 26
Could You Be on the Front Line? 28

Glossary 30
Learning More 31
Index and About the Author 32

PROTECTING PEOPLE

Police officers put their lives in danger every day to serve and protect the communities in which they live and work. Police officers who work together in a specific area are called a police force. A police force is responsible for ensuring public safety at all times. It is a government service that enforces laws. The government gives the police special powers to maintain law and order, make communities safer, reduce people's fear of crime, and improve their quality of life.

AROUND THE CLOCK

Police forces must be available 24 hours a day because emergencies and crimes can happen at any time. Most officers work 40 hours a week. Each shift is about 8 to 10 hours long, but shifts can take place at any time of the day or night and on weekends or holidays. Police officers work in many different environments. Some work indoors. They may sit at a desk and work on a computer. Other officers work outside. They respond to emergencies, such as car accidents and natural disasters. They **investigate** crimes and make arrests. Police officers help out in nonemergency situations when they are needed, too.

The Royal Canadian Mounted Police (RCMP) is Canada's national police force. It enforces laws passed by the Canadian government.

New York City is home to the largest police force in the United States. It has more than 36,000 police officers.

TOP QUALITIES

The best police officers have strong communication skills. They write clear reports after an incident and do not leave out any details. They listen carefully and ask a lot of questions. **Empathy** is an important quality in a police officer. Officers often respond to situations in which people are upset. These people need to believe that the officer understands their situation and truly cares about them. Police officers must also have **integrity**. They need to be seen as trusted members of society.

Your FRONTLINE Career

Look for "Your Frontline Career" boxes. They highlight the skills and strengths needed for specific police careers. They can be used to help you decide whether a career in the police force is for you and what roles might suit you best.

A FRONTLINE CAREER

A police officer is one of the best-known jobs in the world, but there are many types of police officer, and each one has a different role to do. **Recruits** in training are called cadets. As they rise through the **ranks** within the police force, they receive different titles. Ranks vary from one police force to another, but most are similar to military ranks.

DIFFERENT ROLES

Police ranks are based on military ranks. They define authority, chain of command, and responsibility. Chain of command is a system for giving and receiving orders. The word "officer" can be used to describe anyone who works on a police force, but it is also used for the lowest-ranking members on the force. Corporals are one step above officers. They take a leadership role over some of the other officers. Sergeants help with training. They look for ways to improve the workplace and develop new **policies**. Lieutenants hire new staff, create work schedules, assign tasks, **evaluate** other officers, and assist captains. Captains manage specific **divisions** within the police department. They prepare **budgets**, write reports, conduct research, and **monitor** the other officers. The chief of police is the highest-ranking officer. They manage the overall activities of the whole department. Some larger communities also have a police commissioner or superintendent, who oversees all of the different police departments within the area.

There are about 800,000 police officers in the United States. Women account for about 12 percent.

DIFFERENT DIVISIONS

A police force is made up of many separate divisions. Each division is responsible for a specific area. Some divisions are small and have just a few officers, while others are very large and have hundreds of officers. It all depends on the size of the area and the number of people the division serves. Within each division, there are different departments, or stations. They patrol and monitor a certain community within their division. There are also different units within police departments that perform unique activities, such as **community relations** and **special operations**.

The Los Angeles Police Department (LAPD) has one of the best Special Weapons and Tactics (SWAT) teams in the United States.

MAKING A DIFFERENCE

Many police departments work with local youth to help prevent crime. For example, the Arlington Police Department in Texas started the Coach 5–0 program after a high school athlete was killed by a gang member. More than 65 officers join athletes at school for workouts and other activities. Officers **mentor** *the athletes and help them develop the skills to make good choices both in sports and life.*

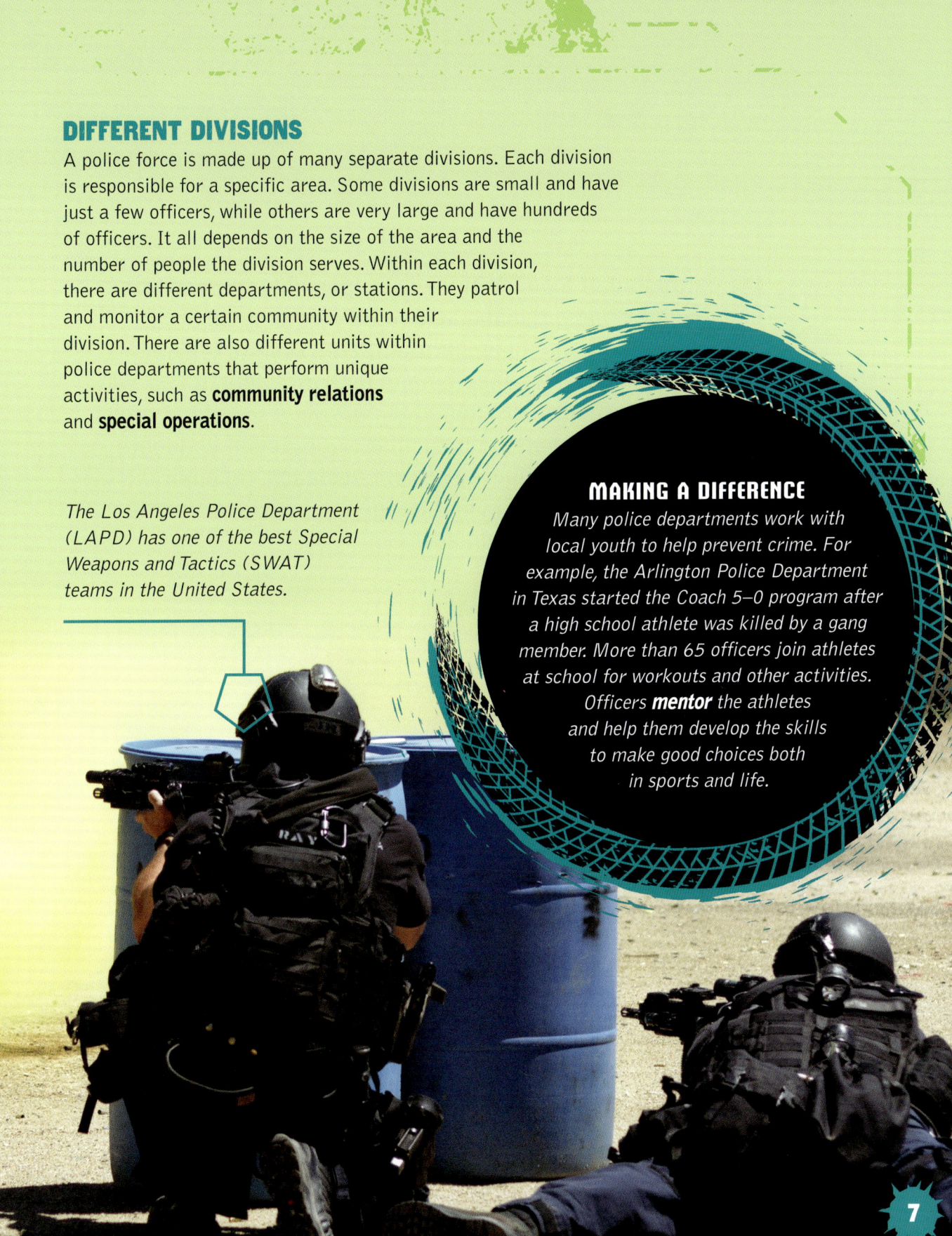

FRONTLINE PATROLLING

The patrol unit of a police force is responsible for monitoring communities and providing an overall sense of security. When a 911 call comes in, patrol officers rush to the scene. They investigate any concerns and look for ways to address them. Patrol officers are trained to perform a variety of tasks because they respond to many different types of incidents each day. They learn how to collect **evidence**, reconstruct accidents to understand what happened, and identify drugs and other harmful substances.

POLICE OFFICERS ON PATROL

Patrol officers' main job is to look for signs of criminal activity in their patrol area. They gather evidence from crime scenes, speak with people, write reports, and arrest **suspects**. They respond to **domestic disputes** or **assault** cases, help victims to safety, and make sure they receive proper medical care, if needed. Patrol officers may direct traffic during special events or if streetlights are not working. They may also hand out tickets to people who break the law, such as speeding drivers.

When patrol officers are not responding to calls, they focus on preventing crime in the communities in which they work.

8

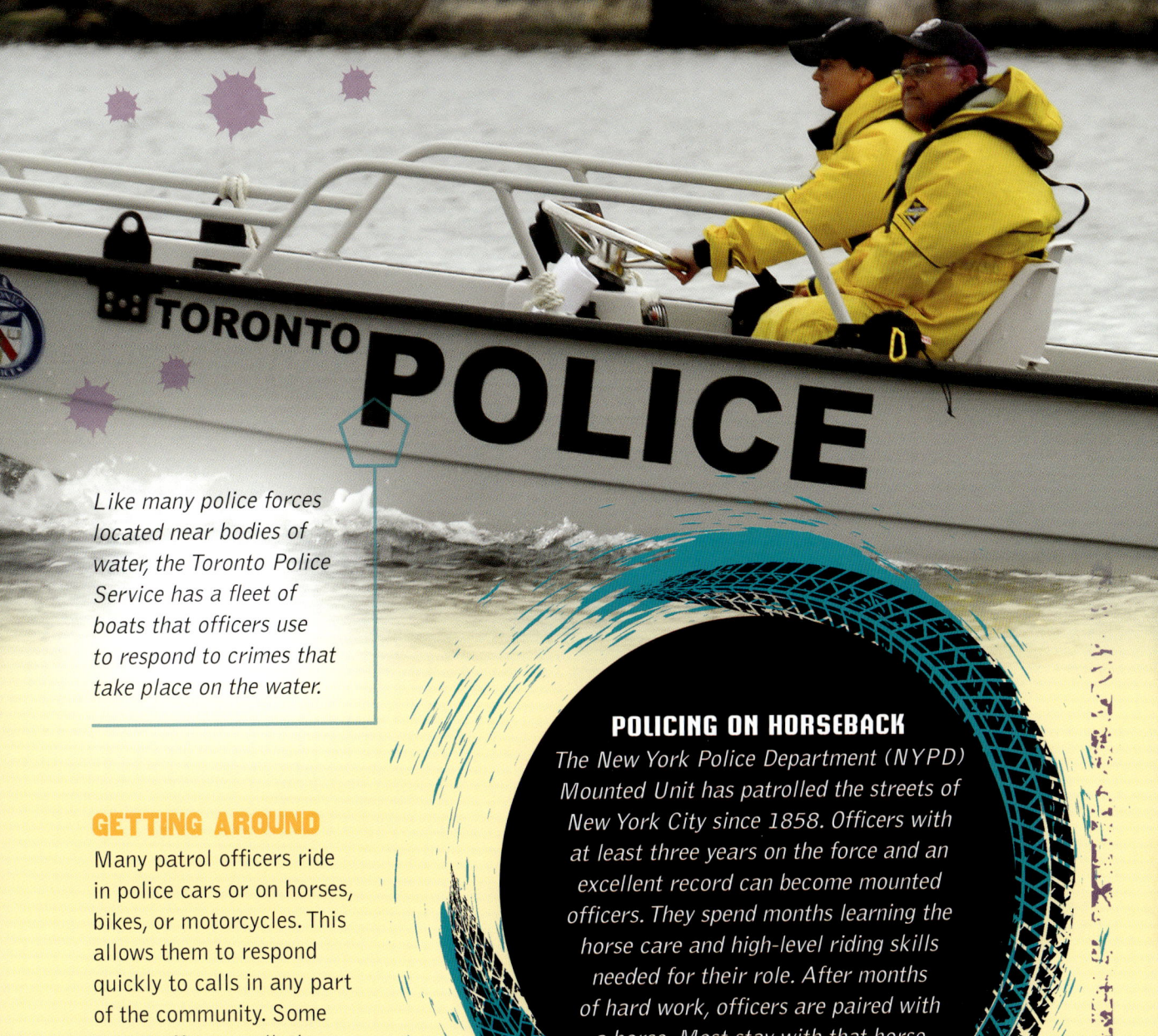

Like many police forces located near bodies of water, the Toronto Police Service has a fleet of boats that officers use to respond to crimes that take place on the water.

GETTING AROUND

Many patrol officers ride in police cars or on horses, bikes, or motorcycles. This allows them to respond quickly to calls in any part of the community. Some patrol officers walk the streets instead. They are known as foot patrol, or beat, officers. Foot patrols mostly work in urban areas or green spaces, such as parks. They get to know the people who live and work in the area. They find out which areas are more **prone** to crime and when crimes are most likely to take place. They make sure they have more of a presence at those times and places. Officers who walk the beat build strong relationships with locals and bring a greater feeling of safety to the communities they serve.

POLICING ON HORSEBACK

The New York Police Department (NYPD) Mounted Unit has patrolled the streets of New York City since 1858. Officers with at least three years on the force and an excellent record can become mounted officers. They spend months learning the horse care and high-level riding skills needed for their role. After months of hard work, officers are paired with a horse. Most stay with that horse for their entire career.

Andrew Youssef: HORSEBACK-RIDING HERO

Mounted police can act fast. Unlike officers on foot or in vehicles, mounted police can quickly cut through parks and across streets to chase after suspects. And that is exactly what NYPD mounted officer Andrew Youssef did when he saw a woman in trouble on the evening of June 20, 2016.

Is Being a Mounted Police Officer for You?

Sounds Great
- Riding a horse every day
- Spending time in parks and at outdoor events
- Providing all kinds of assistance to people in need
- Taking part in parades and special events

Things to Think About
- Having to make quick decisions
- Being ready for action at all times
- Undergoing months of specialized training with horses
- Working in all kinds of weather, such as extreme heat or cold

NYPD mounted police officers are known for their warm, friendly personalities. People often approach them to pet their horses or ask questions about the areas they patrol. While most officers enjoy this part of the job, they need to be ready for action even when they least expect it. Youssef found out firsthand that summer night why it is important to remain on high alert at all times. He was helping a couple with directions when a passerby let him know about a fight at a nearby subway station.

Youssef and his horse, Brooklyn, quickly sprang into action. They arrived in time to see a man running from the subway station. Not long after this, a woman ran out screaming. A man had punched her in the face and stolen her purse. It took only a few minutes for Youssef to realize that the suspect matched the description of the man he had seen running from the station moments earlier.

Mounted officers patrol the streets of Times Square in New York City on horseback.

Youssef called for backup from another mounted officer, David Stagliano, and his horse, Pugsley. Youssef then set off after the suspect. Brooklyn raced through the city streets and soon caught up with the thief. Mounted officers are not allowed to leave their horses alone, so Brooklyn and Youssef nabbed the man together. By then, Stagliano and Pugsley had joined the effort. With his help, Youssef brought the man back to the station. The victim identified the man as her attacker. She was then taken to the hospital for a checkup.

Thanks to Youssef's fast actions and Brooklyn's incredible speed, justice was served, and the suspect was charged with robbery. The two officers were congratulated for a job well done in a social media post from NYPD Special Operations Chief Harry Wedin.

IN THE COMMUNITY

Not all police officers patrol the streets or investigate crimes. Some work in community **outreach programs**. These officers spread awareness of issues in the community. They help educate civilians, or ordinary people, about how they can improve their area, and they look for ways to prevent crimes from taking place. Community relations officers rely on locals to provide information about their communities, so it is important for them to build trusting relationships. These officers need to enjoy interacting with all kinds of people, and they must want to make a difference in the lives of others.

REACHING OUT

Most police stations have one or more community relations officers, depending on the size of the community and the needs of the people they serve. The officers get to know the people in the neighborhoods they serve and provide support where needed. They put a special focus on making **vulnerable** citizens, such as seniors, youth, **LGBTQ**, and minority groups, feel safe. These people are more likely to be bullied, threatened, abused, or robbed. Community relations officers often visit nursing homes, businesses, community centers, and schools. They educate locals about the risks they face and how to protect themselves.

Community relations officers often spend time talking to children. This helps create a sense of trust and respect between the police and youth.

TAKING ACTION

Community relations officers split their time between the station and the communities they serve. They attend community events and give talks. They meet with locals to discuss their concerns and needs. They host youth programs as a way to reduce the chance of teenagers getting involved in crimes or using drugs. Officers often teach safety programs about the dangers in the community. They may give bike safety lessons for children, set up a Crime Stoppers program, or hand out information about how to protect vehicles and homes from burglars.

GAINING TRUST

The city of Durham in North Carolina has a very large Hispanic or Latino population. Some local Hispanics are in the United States illegally. They worry that if they talk to the police, even to report a crime, they might be **deported**. The Durham police created a role on its force to help locals feel safer with the police. The Hispanic **Liaison** Officer takes part in community meetings, workshops, and safety seminars in the hope of getting more members of the Hispanic community to attend and share any concerns they may have with the police.

Some community relations officers provide all-terrain vehicle (ATV) training. They teach people about the rules of riding and how to keep safe.

Sergeant Chris Laush:
BREAKING CULTURAL BARRIERS

In 2012, gang violence and drug dealing were at an all-time high in the Dixon neighborhood of Toronto, Ontario, in Canada. It was common to hear gunshots in the streets and see people selling drugs. Several people were killed in the fighting. The local police knew something had to be done to make the community safer.

Canada has one of the largest Somali populations in the world. Many live in the Dixon Road area of Etobicoke in Toronto and were part of the ongoing gang fighting. Sergeant Chris Laush was tasked with leading a community outreach program aimed at working with Somali locals to help reduce crime. Laush knew the community well. He had worked in the area for most of his career and wanted to help improve the quality of life for locals. As head of the Somali Liaison Unit, Laush knew that his team had to work hard to gain people's trust.

Not long before Laush's team was put in place, the police raided the neighborhood and arrested many people. They laid hundreds of charges, from drug dealing to murder. The raids were supposed to help make the neighborhood safer, but many locals were angry with the police. They thought they could have handled the situation differently. They felt that Somali-Canadians had been treated unfairly. They worried that the rest of the city now only thought of them as criminals.

Is Being a Community Relations Officer for You?

Sounds Great
- Organizing events and working with community volunteers
- Getting to know the people in the community
- Serving as a role model for young people in the community
- Teaching people ways to protect themselves and others in their community

Things to Think About
- May need to help resolve conflicts between people in the community
- Requires strong communication skills
- Can be difficult to build trust with locals

Many Somali-Canadians have a strong sense of **culture**. They often hold community celebrations that express their customs and traditions.

Laush knew that many Somalis did not trust the police. In Somalia, the police are often seen as **corrupt**. Laush and his team wanted to change how Somali locals thought about the police. They began to monitor the Dixon neighborhood daily. They wanted locals to know the police were there if they needed help, and they also knew that crimes were less likely to take place if they were in the area.

Over time, Laush and his team began to form relationships with Somali community members and build their trust. Some members of the unit learned to speak Somali to help improve communication. The unit began to organize youth activities, such as basketball games and field trips. It also helped build a library and computer lab in the area. Today, crime rates among Somalis are much lower since Laush's team was put in place.

INVESTIGATING CRIME

The Crime Investigation Unit works on major crimes, such as **homicides**, kidnappings, **organized crime**, and assaults. Crime investigation officers undergo special training to prepare them for their role. This includes photography, fingerprinting, **blood spatter analysis**, and death scene processing.

ON THE SCENE

Crime scene investigators (CSI) are often the first police officers at a crime scene. Their job is to figure out what happened and who was involved. They look for clues and evidence, such as fingerprints, bloodstains, clothing, weapons, or any other objects that might be important to help solve the case. Officers write down any observations. They take photographs and make drawings to help them recall the details later. They also interview victims, witnesses, and suspects who can help them learn the facts of the case.

READY FOR ACTION

Criminal investigation is a physically demanding, high-stress job. Investigators may find themselves in dangerous or disturbing situations and need to be prepared for anything.

Investigators dust an area with a dye that helps fingerprints stand out when ultraviolet light shines on it.

Crimes take place at all hours of the day or night. Investigators must be on call and ready to work when needed, even on weekends and holidays. Sometimes, investigators work around the clock to solve crimes that put the public at high risk. Every minute counts. The more time that passes, the more likely it is that the crime will not be solved. The crime scene could become **contaminated**, or witnesses might forget some of the details. Officers must be well rested and alert, so that they do not miss any important clues at the scene. Errors can lead to a suspect getting away with the crime.

READING BODY LANGUAGE

Many investigators study body language. Nonverbal cues, such as gestures, the position of the eyes and body, facial expressions, and tone of voice, can tell investigators a lot about a person. Open palms are a sign of honesty, while shoulder shrugging shows confusion, for example. Being able to read body language helps officers know if a suspect is lying. Investigators can also change their own body language to help make a witness or suspect feel at ease and build trust.

Investigators may wear special gear to cover their hair, fingerprints, clothes, and shoes, so that the crime scene is not contaminated.

17

Detective Joe Kenda: HOMICIDE HUNTER

INVESTIGATOR Stories

Detective Joe Kenda is best known as the host of the television show, *Homicide Hunter*. Before gaining fame on the show, Kenda was one of the top criminal investigators in the United States. Kenda's life may seem like something out of a Hollywood thriller, but unlike the movies, the murders he investigated were real.

Kenda became a police officer in 1973, when he joined the Colorado Springs Police Department. He quickly became known for his calm, no-nonsense attitude and his ability to get the job done. Kenda would not stop until he found what he was looking for. But no matter what the situation, Kenda was always nice to people. He found they would give him more information when he treated them well.

Kenda retired from the police force in 1996, but he still thought about his work every day. He drove a special needs school bus for a few years and was happy overall, but something was missing from his life. One day, a television producer asked if he would like to star in a show. Kenda was not interested at first, but his wife pushed him to do it. *Homicide Hunter* first aired in 2011 and ran for nine seasons. During his time on the show, Kenda recreated some of his most chilling murder cases. The show used actual interviews and crime scene reconstructions to tell each story. It revealed how detectives use the powers of reason and observation to put criminals behind bars and give closure to the families of victims.

Your FRONTLINE Career

Is Being a CSI for You?

Sounds Great
- Working environment changes often
- Specializing in a certain type of crime, such as homicide or drug sales
- Piecing together facts
- Being alert and ready for action at all times

Things to Think About
- Crime scenes can be gory and upsetting
- Must be on call all hours of the day and night
- Requires excellent problem-solving skills and good judgment
- Need to pass many fitness tests to qualify for the role

During his time with the Colorado Springs PD, Kenda solved an amazing 92 percent of his cases. The U.S. national average is between 50 and 60 percent. He credits much of his success to his determination. Investigating crimes requires focus, an understanding of the law, and patience. He loved putting pieces of a puzzle together and crime scene investigation fed his natural curiosity. Now, Kenda finds that talking about his cases helps him let go of some of the painful memories that come from murder investigation. Thanks to his role on *Homicide Hunter*, he feels better today than ever before, but he is not done sharing stories of his life's work. He plans to continue to appear on more shows about criminal investigations.

CSI officers such as Kenda are committed to discovering evidence that can help police officers solve crimes, such as homicides.

SPECIAL OPERATIONS

Sometimes, major emergencies take place, such as a **hostage** taking or a bombing. Only certain officers have the skills and qualifications to work on these cases, and they form the Special Operations Bureau (SOB). These officers respond to high-risk incidents that require special training and skills to resolve.

DANGEROUS WORK

Within the SOB, there is a variety of teams or units. Each one specializes in a different area of operation. For example, when the police get a call about a suspicious device, the bomb squad investigates. These officers are trained in all kinds of explosive devices. The Special Weapons and Tactics, or SWAT, team helps with highly specialized tasks, such as hostage rescue, getting past barricades to reach suspects, **sniper** duties, and crowd control. Other uniquely trained members of the Special Operations Unit on a police force include K9 handlers, search and rescue teams, scuba divers, and **crisis negotiation** experts.

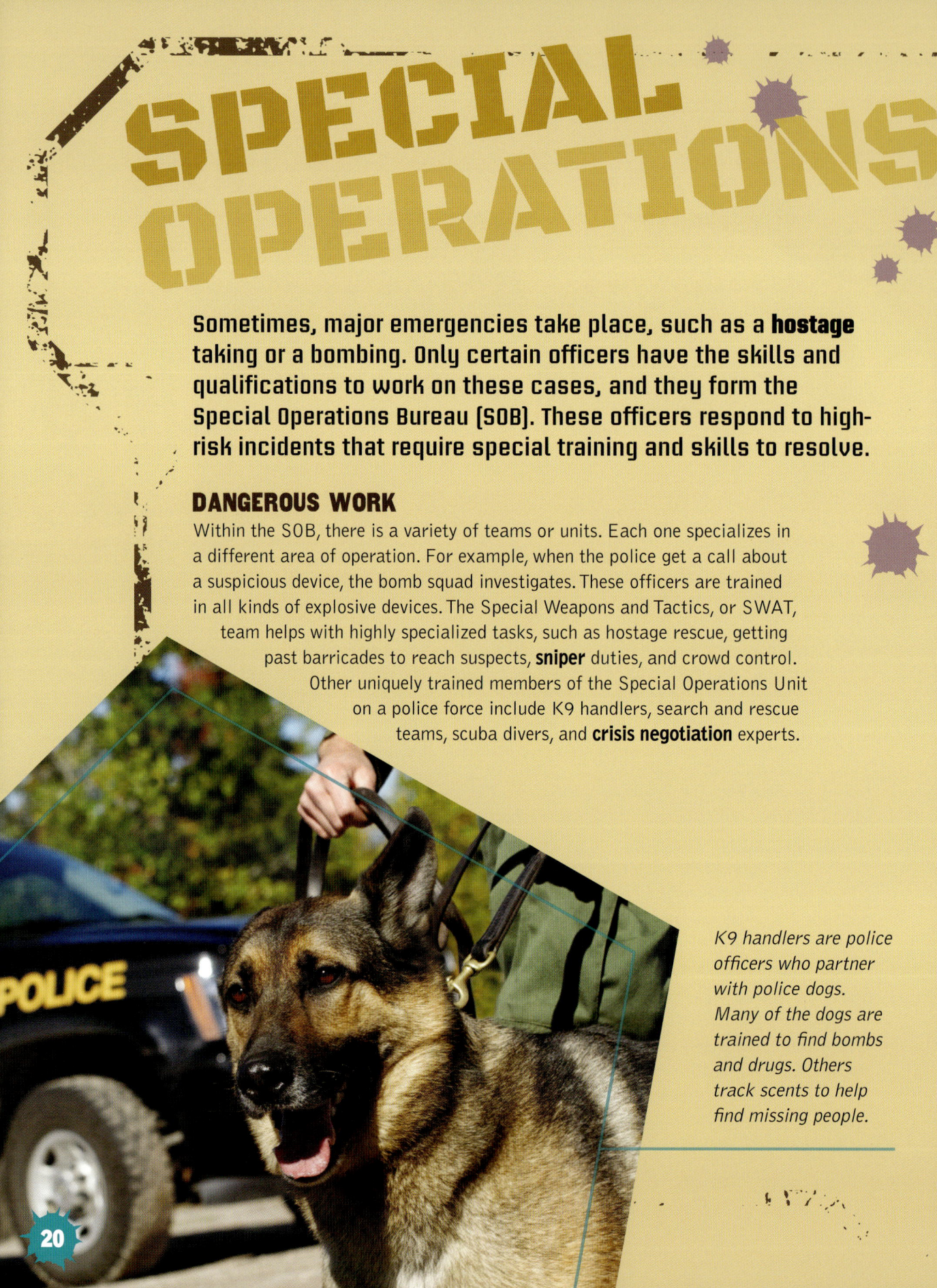

K9 handlers are police officers who partner with police dogs. Many of the dogs are trained to find bombs and drugs. Others track scents to help find missing people.

SWAT teams may use tanks, armor, and military-grade weapons as part of their job.

TOP PERFORMERS

Officers need at least three years of police experience before they can apply for a Special Operations position. They must have an outstanding record of job performance and pass a variety of skills tests. Officers need to show their willingness to work hard. They must promise to keep up a high level of physical fitness. They also must be able to work as part of a team and with very little supervision. If they qualify, officers take part in an advanced training program in which they face intense physical challenges and learn the skills needed for their team. This might include using special weapons, vehicles, or defense techniques.

THE BOSTON BOMB

On April 15, 2013, one of the biggest bomb attacks in U.S. history took place during the Boston Marathon in Massachusetts. In all, 3 people were killed and about 250 others were injured. The local police faced many challenges as the area was too big to keep people from going in or out. They had to check every suspicious bag by hand. This slowed down their investigation. Since then, new measures have been put in place, so that police can act faster if such an event happens again.

Jennifer Grasso: SWAT SUPERSTAR

Jennifer Grasso joined the Los Angeles Police Department (LAPD) in 1995. She started out as a bike patrol officer in a low-crime area. She then moved to an area known for its violent gang activity and was at murder scenes almost every week. Grasso became known for her strong observational skills and her ability to nab drug dealers. From there, her career soared, and Grasso jumped at every chance to take it further.

After 10 years with the LAPD, Grasso joined the elite Metropolitan Division. She worked a number of high-end cases and special assignments, including some that involved the **U.S. Secret Service**. Grasso had always admired the SWAT team but did not think she could join. No other woman ever had. But the Metropolitan Division often worked with the SWAT team. The more Grasso learned about SWAT, the more she wanted to join. SWAT officers did not need to be told what to do. She saw a lot of that in herself.

Grasso was physically very fit, but she began training even harder. She first tried out for the SWAT team in 2007, but she was injured during one of her final physical tests and did not succeed. She tried again in 2008 and was accepted into the 12-week SWAT training program. As a woman, she had to work extra hard to convince the other officers that she was worthy of being on the team.

Is Being in a SWAT Team for You?

Sounds Great
- Exciting and high-energy assignments
- Being trained for a highly specialized role
- Working as part of an elite team
- Using different types of weapons and equipment

Things to Think About
- Must maintain a high level of physical fitness
- Can take years of experience and training to earn a place on the team
- Must be prepared to work in high-risk situations
- Need to be able to make quick decisions under lots of stress

Many did not think Grasso could handle the job and were unkind. But she did not quit. She pushed harder to prove that she could do it. She became the first woman to serve on the LAPD SWAT team and remains the only woman to have done so to date. Over time, the team saw Grasso's talent and began to accept her as one of them.

Grasso spent 10 years on the SWAT team. She handled hundreds of calls each year. She worked as a diver, climber, and emergency medical technician. She also had a special skill at crisis negotiation. Grasso left SWAT when she was promoted to sergeant. She took the opportunity to return to patrolling the streets and share what she learned on SWAT with other members of the force.

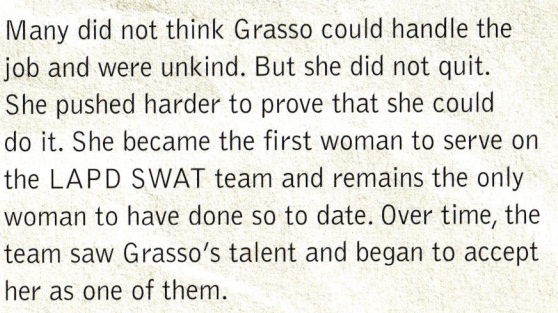

SWAT officers undergo special training to learn how to crawl, climb, or jump into any situation.

BEHIND THE FRONT LINE

Not everyone who works on a police force is a police officer. It takes a team of people behind the scenes to support police officers on the front line. Every police force relies on civilian workers to help its officers do their jobs. **Police dispatchers**, lab analysts, IT specialists, private investigators, **forensic** scientists, and **psychologists** are just a few of the civilian jobs on the police force. They help solve crimes and investigate incidents, but they do not have the power to enforce laws or make arrests.

MIND POWER

Psychologists work with the police in a variety of ways. They help officers maintain their own mental health. This is especially important after an officer experiences a **traumatic** event. Psychologists also help assess the mental health of police recruits. Sometimes, psychologists examine evidence to look for patterns of behavior and create profiles of suspects. Others work with victims to help them through a difficult time. They may also be asked to interview suspects or help with crisis situations. They try to understand what the suspects are thinking and feeling.

Computer specialists make sure that officers have the software and services they need to do their jobs well.

Psychologists help ensure police recruits have the emotional and intellectual skills needed for the job.

SCIENCE AT WORK

Forensic science technicians work at the crime scene to collect weapons, fingerprints, bodily fluids, and other items that might provide clues to the case. They create a list of the evidence and ensure that it is properly stored, so that it does not become contaminated. Then, they use scientific tools and methods to analyze the evidence in a lab. They might look closely at bullets to figure out the type of gun they came from or where the gun was pointing when it was fired. They run tests on blood, **DNA**, and fiber samples to help identify victims or suspects. They write detailed reports of their findings that police officers can use to solve crimes.

DOGS SOLVING CRIMES

Training K9s and handling them requires a lot of experience and hard work. Carren Corcoran is a police officer and dog trainer in Madison, Wisconsin. In 2010, she was partnered with a German shepherd named Slim. Together, Corcoran and Slim have helped solve many crimes. Slim uses his sense of smell and tracking skills to help locate human remains.

SUPPORT Stories

Anastacia Byrne:
SAVING LIVES WITH WORDS

A police dispatcher is one of the most important jobs on a police force. In an emergency, dispatchers are the first line of defense. San Francisco dispatcher Anastacia Byrne helped save lives by keeping people calm and out of harm's way when a shooter entered a United Parcel Service (UPS) distribution facility on June 14, 2017. Byrne's first call of the day was a frightened worker inside the building with the active shooter. The worker had heard gunshots in the hallway and ran into an office. She locked the door, hid behind a desk, and then called 911.

Your FRONTLINE Career

Is Being a Police Dispatcher for You?

Sounds Great
- Responding to a variety of emergency and nonemergency calls
- Multitasking to gather data and dispatch first responders as needed
- Being able to determine which calls are the highest priority
- Acting as a trustworthy source of help to people in stressful situations

Things to Think About
- Must be able to take control of stressful, chaotic, and emotional situations
- Requires excellent attention to detail
- Need strong communication skills to collect and record data from various sources
- Need to keep a calm and level head in high-pressure situations

Byrne kept the caller calm but at the same time tried to gather as much information as she could about the crime scene. She asked questions about whether she could hear any footsteps, voices, or gunshots. She told the caller to push anything she could up against the door and to find something heavy she could use as a weapon if needed. At the same time, Byrne entered all the details she could into the computer system. The information helped officers on the scene know the layout of the building as well as where to look for victims, the shooter, and others in hiding. Byrne stayed on the line with the caller for 20 minutes until help arrived. When she knew the woman was safe, Byrne hung up the phone and picked up the next call.

Emergency dispatchers such as Byrne were the first responders on the scene that day. They provided the police and medics the information they needed to act fast. They helped keep frantic callers safe and prevented more deaths. In the end, although the shooter killed three UPS drivers before killing himself, the death toll could have been much higher had it not been for the calming efforts of Byrne and the other dispatchers. Byrne was later recognized by the San Francisco Department of Emergency Management for her fast and professional response as one of the first 911 dispatchers to receive a call that day. The information she collected from the caller was vital in helping emergency workers quickly respond to the scene and get people to safety.

Dispatchers need to make quick decisions with little knowledge of the situation. They need to be professional and calming when dealing with people who are in high-stress or dangerous situations.

COULD YOU BE ON THE FRONT LINE?

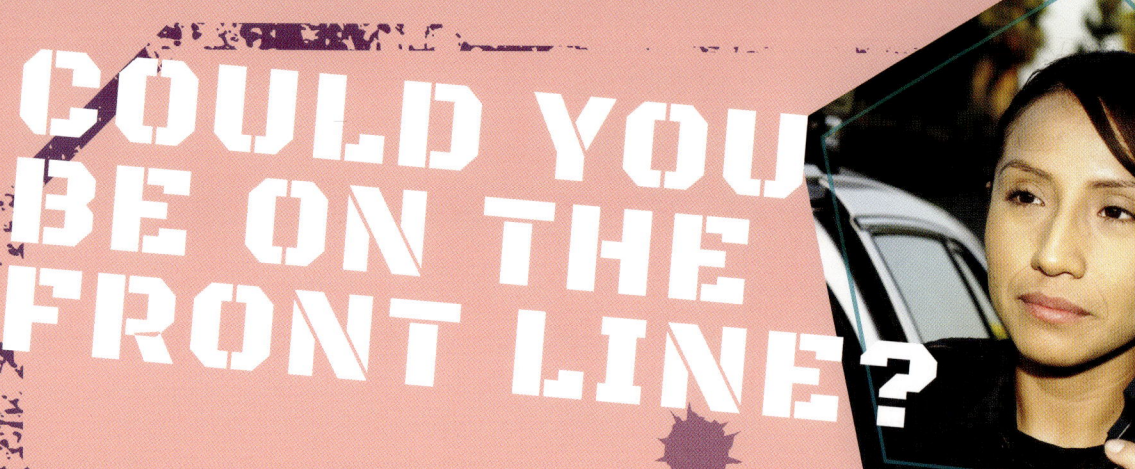

[Do you have what it takes to become a police officer? Here are some of the key things to think about if you want to work on a police force.]

EDUCATION
To apply to become a police officer, you need a high school diploma or GED. Most police jobs also require either a college or university degree, military service, or some type of related job experience. New recruits must attend the police academy to learn the skills needed for the job. Failing even one course can prevent a recruit from working as a police officer. It is important to develop good study habits to prepare for college or university and the police academy.

VALUES
Police officers are expected to have high **moral** and **ethical** standards. They should enjoy working with people and show respect for everyone, no matter what their race, gender, age, or beliefs. Think about the way you behave toward others. Spend time getting to know the people in your community, and build relationships.

FITNESS
Physical and mental fitness are important. Officers need the skills and strength to protect themselves and others from harm. Running laps and doing exercises such as sit-ups and push-ups can help prepare you for police fitness tests.

DEDICATION AND COMMITMENT

Police officers often work long hours, including evenings, weekends, and holidays. They often work overtime, especially if their department is short-staffed. This can take a toll on their health and affect the balance between their work life and the time they spend at home with their family and friends. Ask your family how they feel about you becoming a police officer.

QUALITIES

Police officers need to speak with a wide variety of people and report the details of accidents and investigations. Officers should display maturity, empathy, and **compassion**. They must be open to different perspectives, show a willingness to learn and ask questions at all times, and have a strong desire to help and protect others.

CARVING A CAREER

There are many different job opportunities for police officers and support workers in U.S. and Canadian police forces. Find out about them, and think about what you might like to do.

GLOSSARY

assault A physical attack
blood spatter analysis Study of the pattern of blood to understand a violent crime
budgets Plans of how money should be spent
community relations The relationships an organization builds with people in the area where it is located
compassion Concern for those who are suffering
contaminated Something made less pure by bringing it into contact with other substances or objects
corrupt Immoral or improper conduct
crisis negotiation A police tactic used to communicate with suspects who are threatening violence
culture The religion, art, and way of life of a people or country
deported Forced to leave
divisions Parts of a larger organization
DNA A material found in all living beings that determines how they will look, behave, and function
domestic disputes Situations in which people who live together get into a fight
empathy The ability to sense, understand, and share other people's feelings and emotions
ethical Relating to beliefs about what is right or wrong, and obeying rules and standards
evaluate Determine the worth, importance, or value of something
evidence A collection of facts and information that help prove if something is true or false
forensic Scientific methods and tests used to investigate crimes
homicides Crimes in which one person kills another person
hostage Someone who is held prisoner for money or political reasons
integrity The trait of being fair and honest
investigate Carefully examine a person or situation
LGBTQ An acronym that stands for lesbian, gay, bi, trans, and queer, used to describe people's sexuality

liaison A person who builds and maintains understanding between people
mentor To help someone with advice, especially a younger or less experienced person
monitor To watch over or check on the progress or quality of something over a period of time
moral Concerned with right and wrong behavior and proper conduct
organized crime Complex groups of criminals who work together to commit crimes locally, nationally, and around the world
outreach programs Programs that provide services to people who may not otherwise have access to those services
police dispatchers People who take 911 calls and provide information to the police, so that they can quickly respond to the situation
policies Actions or procedures that guide an organization
prone Likely to happen
psychologists People who study the human mind, emotions, and behavior, so they can help others cope with mental health issues
ranks Positions of an officer
recruits Officers that are new on a police force and are not yet fully trained
sniper A person trained to shoot a target from far away
special operations Military and law enforcement groups that are specially trained to handle complex and dangerous situations
suspects People thought to be guilty of a crime
traumatic Relates to an experience that causes great emotional upset
U.S. Secret Service A branch of the government that does spy work, top secret investigations, and protects important people, such as the president
vulnerable In need of special care or at greater risk from harm or attack

LEARNING MORE

Discover more about the police force and careers on the front line.

BOOKS

Greve, Tom. *SWAT: Special Weapons and Tactics* (Emergency Response). Rourke Educational Media, 2014.

Herweck, Diana. *All in a Day's Work: Police Officer.* Teacher Created Materials, 2013.

Mooney, Carla, and Samuel Carlbaugh. *Forensics: Uncover the Science and Technology of Crime Scene Investigation.* Nomad Press, 2013.

Tisdale, Rachel. *Police Officers.* Crabtree Publishing Company, 2012.

WEBSITES

Discover what it takes to become a K9 officer at:
www.criminaljusticedegreeschools.com/criminal-justice-careers/k9-officer

Learn all about the different types of jobs on a police force at:
www.discoverpolicing.org/explore-the-field/types-of-sworn-law-enforcement

Find out how to become a police officer at:
www.learnhowtobecome.org/police-officer

To learn more about the Royal Canadian Mounted Police, visit:
www.rcmp.gc.ca

For more information about crime scene investigation, visit:
https://learning-center.homesciencetools.com/article/about-forensic-science-csi-for-kids

INDEX

0-9
911 8, 26, 27

A
all-terrain vehicles (ATV) 13
assault 8

B
blood spatter analysis 16
body language 17
Boston Marathon bombing 21
Byrne, Anastacia 26–27

C
Coach 5-0 program 7
communication 5, 14, 26, 27
community relations 7, 12, 13
Corcoran, Carren 25
crime scene investigators (CSI) 16, 17, 18, 19
Crime Stoppers 13
crisis negotiation 20, 23

D
divisions 6, 7
DNA 25
domestic disputes 8

E
evidence 8, 16, 19, 24, 25

F
forensics 16, 17, 18, 19, 24, 25

G
gang violence 14
Grasso, Jennifer 22–23

H
Hispanic Liaison Officer 13
Homicide Hunter 18, 19
homicides 7, 14, 16, 18, 19, 21, 22, 26, 27
hostage taking 20

I
investigators 16, 17, 18, 24

K
K9 handlers 20
Kenda, Joe 18–19

L
Laush, Chris 14–15
LGBTQ 12
Los Angeles Police Department (LAPD) 7, 22, 23

M
medics 27
mental health 24
mounted police 9, 10–11

N
New York Police Department (NYPD) 5, 9, 10, 11

O
organized crime 16
outreach programs 12

P
police dispatchers 24, 26–27
policies 6
psychologists 24

R
recruits 24, 25, 28
Royal Canadian Mounted Police (RCMP) 4

S
snipers 20
Somali Liaison Unit 14, 15
Special Operations Bureau (SOB) 20, 21
Stagliano, David 11
suspects 8, 10, 16, 20, 24, 25
SWAT 7, 20, 21, 22–23

T
Toronto Police Service 9, 14, 15

U
United Parcel Service (UPS) 26, 27
U.S. Secret Service 22

W
Wedin, Harry 11
witnesses 16, 17

Y
Youssef, Andrew 10–11

ABOUT THE AUTHOR

Heather C. Hudak has written hundreds of educational books on all kinds of topics. When she's not writing, Heather enjoys traveling the world or camping in the mountains near her home with her husband and many rescue pets. In researching this book, Heather enjoyed learning about all of the hard work and training that goes into becoming a member of a police force.